How to Qualify for a HELOC

The Step-by-Step Borrower's Playbook to Getting Approved

By Joseph G. Correa

Licensed Mortgage Broker, Finibi Mortgage

Copyright & Legal Notice

First Edition, 2026

Table of Contents

Foreword 5

Chapter 1: The HELOC Qualification Formula: How Banks Decide Yes or No 11

Chapter 2: Income That Gets Approved: How Lenders Really Measure What You Earn 17

Chapter 3: Debt-to-Income Mastery: The Number That Decides How Much You Can Borrow 22

Chapter 4: Credit That Gets Approved: How Scores, Utilization, and Structure Control Your HELOC Outcome 26

Chapter 5: Home Value and Appraisals: How Lenders Decide What Your House Is Worth 30

Chapter 6: Timing, Strategy, and Application Structure: How to Apply So You Actually Get Approved 33

Chapter 7: Stacking Power: How Multiple HELOCs, Lenders, and Properties Multiply Your Approval 36

Chapter 8: How to Get the Maximum HELOC: Optimizing Every Variable Before You Apply 39

Chapter 9: Risk, Reserves, and Bank Psychology: Why Some Borrowers Are Trusted With More 42

Chapter 10: From Application to Approval: The Exact Path Your HELOC Takes Through the Bank 45

Chapter 11: Denials, Appeals, and Second Chances: How to Turn a "No" Into a "Yes" 48

Chapter 12: Your HELOC Readiness Blueprint: How to Know When You Are Guaranteed to Qualify 51

Chapter 13: From Borrower to Power User: How to Use Your First HELOC to Qualify for Bigger Ones 54

Chapter 14: The Long-Term Qualification Strategy: How to Keep Qualifying for Bigger HELOCs for Life 58

Chapter 15: The Ultimate HELOC Qualification System: How to Engineer Your Financial Life for Unlimited Access to Capital 62

Final Thoughts 66

Foreword

Most homeowners assume that qualifying for a home equity line of credit is a mysterious process controlled by banks, algorithms, and credit bureaus that seem to operate behind a closed curtain. Many believe it is purely a matter of having a good credit score or owning a home for a long time. Others assume that if they were denied once, they will always be denied. In reality, HELOC qualification is neither random nor unfair—it is a precise financial equation that can be learned, optimized, and controlled. This book exists to pull back the curtain and show you exactly how that equation works so you can position yourself to win. Once you understand the rules of the system, you no longer feel powerless. You become a strategic borrower, capable of turning your home into a financial engine rather than a trapped asset.

In my work as a licensed mortgage broker, I see people get declined every day for reasons that are completely avoidable. I also see people with average credit, self-employment income, or unconventional financial profiles get approved for large HELOCs simply because their application was structured correctly. Banks do not approve loans based on who deserves them; they approve loans based on risk formulas, income stability, equity, and documentation presentation. Those formulas are rigid, but they are not hidden. When you know what lenders look for, how they verify income, how they calculate risk, and how they view different types of borrowers, you can reverse-engineer your way into approval. This book was written to give you that blueprint.

The most common mistake borrowers make is thinking qualification is about impressing a lender instead of fitting their model. A lender does not care about your hustle, your future plans, or how confident you feel about repaying the loan. They care about what their underwriting system sees today. That system measures your debt-to-income ratio, your credit profile, your equity position, and the consistency of your income in very specific ways. If you do not understand how those variables are calculated, you are guessing. If you do understand them, you can control them. This book will teach you how every major approval factor is calculated, how to strengthen each one, and how to present your financial profile in a way that lenders are built to accept.

Qualifying for a HELOC is not just about getting approved—it is about getting approved for the largest possible line, at the best possible rate, with the most flexible terms. Two borrowers with the same income and credit score can receive drastically different HELOC offers based on how their file is structured. The difference between a $40,000 line and a $250,000 line often comes down to technical details that most homeowners never learn: how income is averaged, how liabilities are counted, how equity is measured, how credit limits affect risk models, and how different banks treat the same borrower. This book shows you how to optimize every one of those variables so you are not leaving money on the table.

Many people believe that qualifying for a HELOC is harder today than it used to be. In some ways that is true—regulations, compliance rules, and automated underwriting have made banks more cautious. But at the same time, new products, alternative documentation programs, and portfolio lenders have created more opportunities than ever before for borrowers who understand how to navigate the system. There are ways for self-employed borrowers, real estate investors, retirees, and even high-net-worth individuals with complex finances to qualify for strong HELOC programs. The key is knowing which programs exist and how to position yourself for them. That is what this book gives you.

This volume is designed as a practical playbook, not a theory guide. You will learn how lenders calculate qualifying income, how they review tax returns, how they analyze bank statements, how they treat business owners, and how they decide what your home is worth. You will learn how credit scores actually influence approval and pricing, and how things like utilization, available credit, and trade-line mix change how lenders see you. You will learn how debt-to-income ratios really work and how to legally and ethically improve them. These are not tricks or loopholes—they are the mechanics of the lending system that professionals use every day.

One of the biggest breakthroughs borrowers experience when they understand qualification is that denial stops feeling personal. When a bank declines a HELOC, it is not a judgment of your character—it is a data mismatch. Something in your financial snapshot does not fit their model. When you know what that mismatch is, you can correct it. You can adjust timing, pay down the right balances, move the right assets, structure income properly, or choose a lender whose model fits your profile better. Suddenly, approval becomes a process instead of a gamble. That shift alone gives you power most homeowners never realize they have.

This book also prepares you for what comes next. Once you qualify for a HELOC, you will have access to one of the most powerful financial tools available to a homeowner. But power without understanding leads to risk. That is why the entire Home Equity Wealth Series is structured in a logical sequence. You begin by understanding how HELOCs work in Book 1. In this book, you learn how to qualify for them. In later volumes, you learn how to use them to invest, eliminate debt, fund businesses, and grow wealth without putting your home in danger. Qualification is the gateway that makes all of that possible.

As a mortgage professional, I can tell you that the borrowers who get the best outcomes are not the ones with the highest incomes or the most expensive homes. They are the ones who understand the system and plan ahead. They know when to apply, how to prepare, and which lenders to approach. They do not walk into the process blind. This book turns you into that kind of borrower. Whether you are a first-time HELOC applicant or someone who has been declined in the past, the knowledge here will give you a clear, strategic path forward.

Your home is likely your largest financial asset. Most people let it sit there quietly, growing in value but never doing anything productive for their lives. When you qualify for a HELOC the right way, that dormant equity becomes accessible capital that can be used to change your financial future. That transformation does not begin when you sign loan documents—it begins when you understand how to qualify. That is why this book matters. It is the bridge between owning a home and using that home as a financial tool.

By the time you finish this volume, you will no longer be guessing about what lenders want. You will know how to prepare, how to position yourself, and how to get approved with confidence. That knowledge alone puts you ahead of the vast majority of homeowners in America. And when you combine it with the strategies that follow in the rest of this series, it gives you something even more valuable: control over your financial destiny through the equity you already own.

Chapter 1

The HELOC Qualification Formula: How Banks Decide Yes or No

Every HELOC approval in America is governed by a formula. It is not emotional, personal, or subjective. It is a mathematical model that evaluates risk using four primary pillars: home equity, income, credit, and debt. When those four numbers fit inside the lender's tolerance, you get approved. When they do not, you are declined, regardless of how much money you make or how long you have owned your home. The first step to mastering HELOC qualification is understanding that you are not being judged as a person—you are being evaluated as a balance sheet.

The first and most important factor is equity. Equity is the difference between what your home is worth and what you owe on it. Lenders do not lend against the purchase price or what you think your home is worth; they lend against what their appraisal or automated valuation model determines. Most HELOC lenders will allow a combined loan-to-value ratio, called CLTV, between 80 percent and 90 percent depending on the bank, the borrower, and the market. This means that if your home is worth $500,000 and your lender allows 85 percent CLTV, the maximum total debt allowed on your home is $425,000. If you already owe $300,000 on your first mortgage, the maximum HELOC you could qualify for is $125,000. That number is not negotiable—it is a hard mathematical limit.

The second pillar is income. Lenders are not interested in how much you think you earn; they are interested in what they can document and verify. W-2 employees are evaluated based on gross income from pay stubs and tax returns. Self-employed borrowers are evaluated based on net income after expenses, usually averaged over two years. Bank statement programs may use deposits instead. Retirees may use Social Security, pensions, and investment income. What matters is not how much money flows through your life, but how much stable, recurring income the lender can legally count.

The third pillar is debt. Lenders calculate something called a debt-to-income ratio, or DTI. This compares your monthly debt obligations to your gross monthly income. Most HELOC lenders require a DTI below 43 percent, though some allow up to 50 percent. This means if you make $10,000 per month, your total monthly obligations—including your mortgage, property taxes, insurance, car payments, credit cards, student loans, and the new HELOC payment—must usually be below $4,300 to $5,000. This is one of the most misunderstood numbers in lending. A borrower can make six figures and still be denied because their debt is too high. The fourth pillar is credit. Credit determines both approval and pricing. A borrower with a 760 score may qualify for 90 percent CLTV and the lowest rates. A borrower with a 660 score may be limited to 80 percent CLTV with higher rates. Credit also affects whether a lender will even consider your application. Late payments, collections, high balances, and short credit history all reduce approval probability. However, many borrowers are surprised to learn that small strategic changes—such as paying down balances or increasing credit limits—can dramatically improve their profile within weeks.

What ties all four pillars together is risk. Banks are not afraid of lending; they are afraid of losing money. Every underwriting rule exists to limit the chance of default. When your equity is high, your income is stable, your debts are controlled, and your credit is strong, the lender sees you as safe. When any one of those variables is weak, the system flags risk. Understanding this lets you stop guessing and start engineering your approval.

The reason this matters so much is that HELOCs are revolving credit lines. Unlike fixed second mortgages, lenders know you can draw more money in the future. That makes them more cautious. They are not just approving today's balance—they are approving your potential future borrowing. That is why

HELOC underwriting is stricter than many people expect, and why preparing correctly before applying can make the difference between a denial and a six-figure credit line.

Once you understand this formula, qualifying becomes a project instead of a mystery. You can increase equity by choosing the right valuation method. You can increase income by timing applications around bonuses, raises, or tax returns. You can reduce DTI by paying off or restructuring debts. You can improve credit by reducing utilization and correcting errors. Every one of these moves changes the equation in your favor. That is what this book is designed to help you do.

Practical Example: *How a Borrower Qualifies for a $140,000 HELOC*

Maria owns a home in Orlando, Florida. Her home was purchased five years ago for $350,000. Today, similar homes in her neighborhood are selling for about $500,000. She applies for a HELOC. The lender orders an appraisal, which comes back at $500,000. Maria still owes $290,000 on her first mortgage. The bank allows an 85 percent combined loan-to-value ratio. To calculate her maximum allowed debt, the bank multiplies $500,000 by 0.85, which equals $425,000. This is the maximum total amount that can be owed against her home.

Next, the lender subtracts Maria's existing mortgage from that $425,000 limit. $425,000 minus $290,000 equals $135,000. That means the largest HELOC Maria can possibly receive from this bank is $135,000. This number is purely mathematical. No amount of income or credit can push it higher unless the home appraises for more or the bank allows a higher CLTV.

Now the lender evaluates Maria's income. She works full-time and earns $96,000 per year. Dividing $96,000 by 12 gives her a gross monthly income of $8,000. The lender then reviews her monthly debts. Her mortgage payment is $2,100. Her car payment is $500. Her credit cards have a minimum total payment of $400. She has no student loans. Her total monthly debt before the HELOC is $3,000.

The lender then calculates the potential HELOC payment. Most banks estimate this using an interest-only payment at current rates. Let's assume the HELOC interest rate is 8 percent. An 8 percent annual rate on $135,000 equals $10,800 per year. Dividing that by 12 gives a monthly payment of $900. The lender adds this to Maria's existing $3,000 in debts, giving her a total monthly obligation of $3,900.

Now the lender calculates Maria's debt-to-income ratio. They divide her total monthly debt of $3,900 by her gross monthly income of $8,000. $3,900 divided by $8,000 equals 0.4875, or 48.75 percent. If the lender's maximum allowed DTI is 50 percent, Maria qualifies. If the lender's maximum is 43 percent, she would be denied or offered a smaller HELOC. Assume this lender allows 50 percent DTI. Maria passes the income test. Next, the lender checks her credit. Maria has a 720 credit score, no late payments in the past two years, and low utilization. This qualifies her for the bank's standard HELOC program with 85 percent CLTV. Everything lines up: equity, income, debt, and credit.

As a result, Maria is approved for a $135,000 HELOC. If she had paid off her car loan, reducing her monthly debt by $500, her DTI would drop to $3,400 divided by $8,000, or 42.5 percent, making her eligible even at stricter banks. If her home appraised at $520,000 instead of $500,000, her 85 percent cap would rise to $442,000, increasing her HELOC limit. This example shows how small changes in numbers can create tens of thousands of dollars in available credit.

This is how HELOC qualification really works. It is not luck. It is math. And when you know how the math works, you can control the outcome.

Chapter 2

Income That Gets Approved: How Lenders Really Measure What You Earn

Most homeowners believe that income is simply how much money they make. In lending, income is not defined by what you earn, but by what can be proven, averaged, and relied upon. This distinction is the reason many high-earning borrowers are denied while others with far less income are approved. HELOC lenders do not lend based on potential, optimism, or business growth. They lend based on documented stability. This chapter will teach you how lenders view income, how they calculate it, and how you can structure your financial life to maximize what counts when applying for a HELOC.

For W-2 employees, income is typically calculated using recent pay stubs, W-2 forms, and tax returns. If you are salaried, the lender usually takes your current gross pay and multiplies it by 12 to determine annual income. If you are hourly or commission-based, lenders may average the past 12 to 24 months of earnings. Bonuses, overtime, and commissions may be included, but only if they are consistent and documented over time. A borrower who receives large but irregular bonuses may not be able to count them, even if they are significant.

Lenders are not interested in peak income; they are interested in dependable income.

Self-employed borrowers are evaluated very differently. Instead of gross revenue, lenders look at net income after expenses, as shown on tax returns. This is where many entrepreneurs are caught off guard. A business owner may bring in $300,000 per year, but if their tax returns show only $60,000 in net profit after deductions, that is the number lenders use. Depreciation, vehicle write-offs, and aggressive tax strategies may reduce taxes, but they also reduce qualifying income. When applying for a HELOC, what helps with taxes often hurts with lending.

Some lenders offer bank statement programs for self-employed borrowers. Instead of using tax returns, they analyze deposits into business or personal accounts over a 12- to 24-month period. They then apply an expense factor, often 50 percent, to estimate income. This allows business owners who reinvest or write off large expenses to qualify for much higher HELOC amounts. However, bank statement loans typically have higher interest rates and may require more equity. Choosing the right income documentation method can be the difference between qualifying and being declined.

Retirees and investors often qualify using non-traditional income sources. Social Security, pensions, annuities, rental income, dividends, and interest income can all be used if they are documented and expected to continue. Rental income is usually calculated by taking the rent, subtracting a vacancy factor, and then subtracting the mortgage payment. Only the remaining cash flow counts. Investment income may be averaged over time. Even large asset balances can sometimes be converted into qualifying income using asset-based formulas.

The key concept across all borrower types is stability. Lenders prefer income that is predictable, recurring, and likely to continue for at least three years. Job changes, industry shifts, declining revenue, or recent business startups can reduce qualifying income even if total earnings are high. That is why timing matters. Applying for a HELOC right after switching jobs, starting a business, or restructuring finances can result in a lower approval amount than waiting until income stabilizes.

Understanding how income is counted gives you leverage. You can choose when to apply, how to file taxes, whether to use bank statements, and how to structure payments to yourself. You can decide whether to show more income one year to qualify for a larger HELOC, then optimize taxes later. When you treat income as a strategic variable instead of a fixed fact, you gain control over your borrowing power.

Practical Example: *How Income Determines HELOC Approval*

James owns a home valued at $600,000. He owes $350,000 on his first mortgage. The lender allows an 85 percent CLTV. The maximum total debt allowed is $600,000 multiplied by 0.85, which equals $510,000. Subtracting the $350,000 mortgage leaves $160,000 as the maximum possible HELOC. Now the lender must determine whether James's income supports this amount.

James is self-employed. His business generates $250,000 per year in revenue. On his tax return, after expenses, his net income is $70,000. The lender divides $70,000 by 12, giving a gross monthly income of $5,833. James's monthly debts include a $2,300 mortgage, a $600 car payment, and $300 in credit cards, totaling $3,200. The HELOC interest-only payment on $160,000 at 8 percent is $12,800 per year, or $1,067 per month. Adding this to his existing $3,200 gives $4,267 in total monthly obligations.

To calculate DTI, the lender divides $4,267 by $5,833. This equals 0.731, or 73 percent. This is far above the allowed limit. Even though James earns $250,000 in revenue, his tax returns make him appear risky. He is denied. James instead applies using a bank statement HELOC program. The lender reviews 12 months of deposits, which average $20,800 per month. The lender applies a 50 percent expense factor, leaving $10,400 per month in qualifying income. James's debts remain $3,200, and the HELOC payment is still $1,067, giving total obligations of $4,267. Dividing $4,267 by $10,400 equals 41 percent. This is within the lender's limits. James qualifies for the full $160,000 HELOC.

This example shows how income documentation changes everything. The money James made did not change. Only how it was calculated changed. Understanding that difference allows borrowers to unlock tens or hundreds of thousands of dollars in home equity that would otherwise be inaccessible.

Chapter 3

Debt-to-Income Mastery: The Number That Decides How Much You Can Borrow

Of all the numbers used in HELOC underwriting, none is more important than debt-to-income ratio. This single calculation determines whether you qualify at all and how large your HELOC can be. Many homeowners focus on credit scores and home value, yet are denied because of DTI. The reason is simple: lenders are not afraid of lending against houses; they are afraid of lending to borrowers who are stretched too thin. Your DTI tells the lender how much financial breathing room you have every month.

Debt-to-income ratio is calculated by dividing your total monthly debt by your gross monthly income. Total monthly debt includes your mortgage, property taxes, homeowner's insurance, HOA fees, car payments, student loans, minimum credit card payments, personal loans, and the projected HELOC payment. Gross monthly income is your income before taxes and deductions. If you earn $120,000 per year, your gross monthly income is $10,000. If your total debts add up to $4,000 per month, your DTI is $4,000 divided by $10,000, or 40 percent. Most HELOC lenders want this number below 43 percent, though some allow up to 50 percent. That means even high-income borrowers can be denied if they carry too much debt. A homeowner earning $200,000 per year could be declined while someone earning $80,000 is approved simply because their debt structure is cleaner. This is why DTI is the most controllable and the most powerful variable in HELOC qualification.

Understanding what counts as debt is critical. Many borrowers are shocked to discover that even unused credit cards create DTI impact if they have balances. Lenders use the minimum monthly payment listed on your credit report, not what you choose to pay. Student loans may be counted using either the actual payment or a percentage of the balance. Installment loans such as cars and personal loans count in full. Even co-signed debts count, even if someone else is paying them.

The HELOC itself also counts. Even though it is a line of credit, lenders assume a hypothetical payment when calculating DTI. They usually take the full line amount and apply an interest-only payment using current interest rates. This means a large HELOC increases your DTI even if you have not drawn any money yet. That is why some borrowers qualify for a smaller HELOC but are denied for a larger one. The size of the line itself affects approval. This gives you tremendous strategic leverage. If you reduce your debts before applying, you increase how much HELOC you can qualify for. Paying off a $500 car payment is often more powerful than increasing income by thousands of dollars. Eliminating a credit card with a $100 minimum payment can raise your borrowing capacity by tens of thousands of dollars. When you view debt as a lever instead of a burden, you start making smarter financial decisions.

Timing also matters. Applying right after you pay off a loan or before taking on a new one can change your DTI dramatically. Even a few days can make a difference if your credit report updates. Strategic borrowers plan their HELOC application around these updates to maximize approval.

DTI is not about being debt-free. It is about being balanced. A homeowner with a mortgage, a car, and a HELOC can still qualify if the numbers make sense. The key is understanding how those numbers interact and shaping them to fit within the lender's rules.

Practical Example: *How DTI Controls Your HELOC Size*

Angela owns a home valued at $700,000. She owes $400,000 on her first mortgage. Her lender allows an 85 percent CLTV. The maximum total debt allowed is $700,000 multiplied by 0.85, which equals $595,000. Subtracting her $400,000 mortgage leaves $195,000 as the maximum possible HELOC.

Now the lender must determine whether her income supports that amount.

Angela earns $120,000 per year, which is $10,000 per month. Her existing debts are a $2,600 mortgage payment, a $700 car payment, $300 in credit card minimums, and $400 in student loans. Her total monthly debt before the HELOC is $4,000.

The HELOC payment on $195,000 at 8 percent interest is $15,600 per year, or $1,300 per month. The lender adds this to her $4,000 in existing debt, giving a total of $5,300. To calculate DTI, the lender divides $5,300 by $10,000, resulting in 53 percent. The lender's maximum allowed DTI is 45 percent. Angela is denied.

Angela then pays off her car loan and one credit card, reducing her monthly debt by $900. Her new debt is $3,100. The HELOC payment is still $1,300, so total debt becomes $4,400. Dividing $4,400 by $10,000 gives 44 percent. Now she qualifies.

By eliminating just $900 per month in debt, Angela unlocked nearly $200,000 in home equity. This example shows why debt management is the most powerful HELOC qualification strategy of all.

Chapter 4

Credit That Gets Approved: How Scores, Utilization, and Structure Control Your HELOC Outcome

Credit is not simply a number; it is a risk map of your financial behavior. When a lender reviews your HELOC application, they are not only looking at your credit score but also at the structure behind it. Two borrowers can both have a 720 score and receive very different HELOC outcomes based on how their credit is built. Lenders analyze payment history, balances, credit limits, account age, and the types of credit you use. Understanding how these elements interact allows you to engineer your profile for approval and for the largest possible credit line at the lowest rate.

The most powerful component of your credit profile is payment history. Late payments, collections, charge-offs, and bankruptcies create a risk signal that cannot be ignored. HELOC lenders are particularly sensitive to housing-related delinquencies such as late mortgage payments or prior foreclosures. Even one recent late payment can reduce the maximum CLTV a lender will allow. While you cannot erase the past, you can control how recent negative events are and how your current accounts behave. Twelve to twenty-four months of perfect payment history dramatically increases approval odds.

The second major driver is utilization, which is the percentage of your available credit that you are using. If you have $50,000 in credit limits and carry $25,000 in balances, your utilization is 50 percent. Most HELOC lenders want to see this below 30 percent, and ideally below 10 percent. High utilization signals financial stress even if payments are made on time. Lowering utilization is one of the fastest ways to raise a score and reduce perceived risk. Paying down balances or increasing credit limits can change this ratio within weeks.

Credit structure also matters. Lenders like to see a mix of installment loans and revolving credit. A borrower with only credit cards and no long-term accounts may be seen as riskier than someone with a mortgage, a car loan, and a few credit cards. Length of credit history is also important. Older accounts show stability. Closing old accounts, even if they are unused, can hurt your profile by reducing average age and available credit.

HELOC lenders also look at how many accounts you have and how many inquiries you have recently made. Too many recent credit applications suggest financial distress. Even if your score is high, multiple inquiries and new accounts in a short period can trigger a denial. Strategic borrowers avoid opening new accounts for at least three to six months before applying for a HELOC.

What many homeowners do not realize is that credit impacts not just approval but how much equity you can access. A borrower with excellent credit may be allowed to go to 90 percent CLTV, while a borrower with weaker credit may be capped at 80 percent. On a $600,000 home, that difference is $60,000 in borrowing power. Credit is therefore not just about getting approved; it is about maximizing what you can unlock.

By managing utilization, payment history, account age, and application timing, you can dramatically improve your HELOC outcome. Credit is one of the few variables you can change quickly, which makes it one of the most powerful tools in HELOC planning.

Practical Example: *How Credit Structure Changes HELOC Approval*

David owns a home worth $550,000. He owes $320,000 on his first mortgage. One lender allows 90 percent CLTV for borrowers with strong credit and 80 percent for borrowers with average credit. At 90 percent, the maximum total debt allowed is $550,000 multiplied by 0.90, which equals $495,000. Subtracting David's $320,000 mortgage leaves

$175,000 as the possible HELOC. At 80 percent, the maximum is $550,000 multiplied by 0.80, which equals $440,000. Subtracting $320,000 leaves only $120,000. His credit determines which limit he gets.

David's credit score is 710, but he has $40,000 in credit card limits and $28,000 in balances, giving him 70 percent utilization. He also has two recent late payments from last year. The lender classifies him as average risk and limits him to 80 percent CLTV. He is approved for $120,000.

David then pays down his balances to $8,000, lowering utilization to 20 percent. He also waits 12 months with perfect payments. His score rises to 760. Now the lender qualifies him for 90 percent CLTV. The same house and same mortgage now produce a $175,000 HELOC. By restructuring his credit, David unlocked $55,000 in additional home equity.

Chapter 5

Home Value and Appraisals: How Lenders Decide What Your House Is Worth

When homeowners think about qualifying for a HELOC, they usually focus on income and credit. In reality, the value of the home is just as important, because it determines how much equity even exists to borrow against. You cannot qualify for money that the lender does not believe exists. That is why understanding how home value is calculated, verified, and sometimes challenged is one of the most powerful skills a borrower can have when applying for a HELOC.

Lenders do not rely on Zillow, Redfin, or what your neighbor sold for. They rely on valuation systems designed to protect the bank. These include automated valuation models, drive-by appraisals, and full interior appraisals. Each method produces a different level of precision. Automated valuations are based on recent sales data and statistical modeling. They are fast but conservative. Drive-by appraisals involve a licensed appraiser evaluating the exterior and market data. Full appraisals involve interior inspection and provide the highest values when homes are well maintained or upgraded. Knowing which method your lender uses can affect tens of thousands of dollars in available HELOC funds.

The lender's goal is not to give you the highest possible value; it is to protect against market risk. If prices decline, the bank still wants to be covered. That is why appraisals are often lower than what homeowners expect. However, borrowers who prepare properly can influence this number. Repairs, upgrades, cleanliness, curb appeal, and documentation of recent improvements all help. A clean, updated home with records of renovations almost always appraises higher than one that looks neglected, even if both are structurally similar.

Market conditions also matter. In rising markets, lenders may allow higher CLTV ratios. In declining or volatile markets, they may reduce them. This means two borrowers with identical homes can receive different HELOC offers based on timing and geography. Understanding this helps you choose when to apply and which lender to use.

Valuation disputes are another area where informed borrowers win. If an appraisal comes in low, it is not always final. Lenders often allow reconsiderations if you provide evidence of better comparable sales, renovations, or errors. Many homeowners walk away when an appraisal is low. Strategic borrowers fight it, often successfully.

Your home's value is not fixed. It is a number that can be

influenced. When you understand how lenders determine it, you can maximize your equity and therefore maximize your borrowing power.

Practical Example: *How Home Value Changes HELOC Size*

Sophia owns a home she bought for $420,000 five years ago. She owes $280,000 on her mortgage. Recent sales in her area suggest her home could be worth between $550,000 and $600,000 depending on condition. She applies for a HELOC.

The lender orders an automated valuation, which estimates her home at $550,000. The bank allows 85 percent CLTV. $550,000 multiplied by 0.85 equals $467,500. Subtracting her $280,000 mortgage leaves $187,500 as her maximum HELOC.

Sophia then switches to a lender that orders a full appraisal. The appraiser notes her renovated kitchen, new roof, and upgraded bathrooms. The home appraises at $600,000. 85 percent of $600,000 is $510,000. Subtracting the $280,000 mortgage leaves $230,000. By choosing the right valuation method, Sophia gained $42,500 in additional HELOC capacity.

Chapter 6

Timing, Strategy, and Application Structure: How to Apply So You Actually Get Approved

Most homeowners believe HELOC approval happens at the moment they apply. In reality, approval is decided weeks or even months earlier, based on how well their financial profile was prepared before the application was ever submitted. Timing, structure, and sequencing matter just as much as income, credit, and equity. Two identical borrowers applying on different dates or through different channels can receive completely different results. This chapter explains how to approach the HELOC process like a professional borrower instead of a hopeful applicant.

The first strategic variable is timing. Lenders evaluate income based on what is documented at the time of application. If you are about to receive a raise, bonus, commission spike, or profitable quarter in your business, waiting can significantly increase qualifying income. Conversely, applying right after a job change, business startup, or income dip can reduce or eliminate approval. Even tax filing timing matters. A self-employed borrower who files a low-income tax return in April may be far worse off than if they had applied in March using the prior year's stronger numbers.

Credit timing is equally important. Scores and utilization update as accounts report to the credit bureaus. Paying off a card today does not help if it has not yet reported. Opening new accounts or making major purchases can hurt you for months. Strategic borrowers wait until their balances are low, utilization is optimal, and recent inquiries have aged before submitting a HELOC application.

Another overlooked variable is lender selection. Not all banks use the same formulas. One lender may allow 90 percent CLTV, another only 80 percent. One may use aggressive income calculations, another conservative ones. Some allow bank statements, others do not. Some ignore student loans, others do not. Applying to the wrong lender can mean denial even when you qualify elsewhere. This is why working with a broker who knows which lenders match your profile is so powerful.

Application structure also matters. How income is labeled, which accounts are included, how liabilities are explained, and even the order of documents affects underwriting. Underwriters are trained to look for risk. Clean, well-organized files get approved faster and more generously than messy, confusing ones. The same numbers presented clearly can get a better result than when presented poorly. HELOC approval is not about luck. It is about preparation, sequencing, and choosing the right doorway into the lending system. Borrowers who understand this almost always outperform those who simply apply and hope.

Practical Example: *How Timing and Strategy Change a HELOC Outcome*

Robert owns a home worth $650,000 and owes $360,000. At 85 percent CLTV, his maximum total debt is $552,500. Subtracting his mortgage leaves $192,500 as the maximum HELOC. His income is $110,000 per year, or $9,167 per month. His debts are $2,700 mortgage, $600 car, and $300 credit cards, totaling $3,600.

A $192,500 HELOC at 8 percent creates a $1,283 monthly payment. Total obligations become $4,883. Dividing $4,883 by $9,167 gives 53 percent DTI, which is too high. Robert is denied.

Robert waits three months. During that time, he pays off his car loan, reducing his debt by $600. His new monthly debt is $3,000. He also receives a raise to $125,000 per year, increasing his monthly income to $10,417. Now his HELOC payment is still $1,283, and total debt is $4,283. Dividing $4,283 by $10,417 gives 41 percent DTI. He now qualifies for the full $192,500. Strategic timing turned a denial into a six-figure approval.

Chapter 7

Stacking Power: How Multiple HELOCs, Lenders, and Properties Multiply Your Approval

Most homeowners assume they can only have one HELOC. In reality, many high-level borrowers use multiple HELOCs across different lenders and properties to dramatically increase their access to capital. Banks do not look at you globally; they look at each loan individually. This creates opportunities for borrowers who understand how to structure their applications, sequence lenders, and allocate equity across multiple assets. This chapter explains how HELOC stacking works and how to do it safely and legally.

Each lender evaluates only the property they are lending against. If you own two homes, each can support its own HELOC. Even on a single property, different lenders may offer different CLTV limits, different valuations, and different risk models. One lender may cap you at 80 percent CLTV, while another allows 90 percent. When you apply to the right lender first, you lock in the highest possible position on the title. Subsequent lenders then evaluate the remaining equity. This is where sequencing matters. The lender with the highest CLTV and best valuation should always go first. That lender gets the strongest lien position and gives you the biggest line. After that, other lenders can sometimes place second or even third HELOCs behind it, provided enough equity remains. This is how sophisticated borrowers access far more capital than those who simply go to their local bank.

HELOC stacking is not reckless when done properly. Each lender calculates risk independently. As long as you remain within total allowable CLTV and your income supports the combined payments, the loans are legitimate. The key is controlling total leverage and making sure cash flow supports the debt.

This strategy is especially powerful for real estate investors. Equity from one property can fund the acquisition of another, which then creates new equity and new HELOC opportunities. Over time, this creates a self-reinforcing capital engine.

Practical Example: *How HELOC Stacking Multiplies Borrowing Power*

Laura owns two homes. Her primary home is worth $600,000 with a $300,000 mortgage. Her rental property is worth $400,000 with a $200,000 mortgage. On her primary home, one lender allows 90 percent CLTV. Ninety percent of $600,000 is $540,000. Subtracting her $300,000 mortgage leaves $240,000. She takes a $240,000 HELOC. Another lender allows a second HELOC up to 80 percent CLTV. Eighty percent of $600,000 is $480,000. Subtracting the $300,000 first mortgage and the $240,000 first HELOC leaves negative equity, so no second HELOC is allowed on the primary home.

On her rental property, a lender allows 80 percent CLTV. Eighty percent of $400,000 is $320,000. Subtracting the $200,000 mortgage leaves $120,000. Laura now has $240,000 plus $120,000, totaling $360,000 in HELOC access across two properties. This is how stacking turns equity into a powerful financial engine.

Chapter 8

How to Get the Maximum HELOC: Optimizing Every Variable Before You Apply

Most homeowners think HELOC approval is binary: you either qualify or you do not. In reality, the true game is not just qualifying, but qualifying for the largest possible line at the best possible rate and with the most flexible terms. The difference between an average HELOC and an optimized HELOC can easily be $100,000 or more. That difference comes from controlling every variable in the underwriting formula before you apply.

The first variable to optimize is equity. Equity is not just how much you owe; it is how your home is valued by the lender. Strategic borrowers choose lenders that use the most favorable valuation method, time their applications when prices are rising, and prepare their homes so appraisals come in high. A ten percent increase in appraised value on a $600,000 home creates $60,000 in new equity. When multiplied by an 85 or 90 percent CLTV, that becomes real borrowing power.

Income is the second variable. Borrowers who rely on W-2 income may time their application after raises, promotions, or bonus months. Self-employed borrowers may choose whether to use tax returns or bank statements based on which produces the higher qualifying income. Investors may time applications after rent increases or after refinancing properties. The goal is not to manipulate income but to choose the documentation window that shows your strongest financial position.

Debt is the third variable. Because DTI is a limiting factor, paying off or restructuring debts before applying is one of the fastest ways to increase HELOC size. Even a small reduction in monthly payments can unlock tens of thousands of dollars in additional borrowing. Strategic borrowers focus on eliminating high-payment, low-balance debts such as car loans or credit cards before applying.

Credit is the fourth variable. Raising a score from 680 to 740 can mean the difference between 80 percent and 90 percent CLTV. It can also lower interest rates, which reduces the HELOC payment and improves DTI. This creates a powerful feedback loop: better credit leads to lower payments, which leads to higher approval amounts.

When all four variables are optimized together, the HELOC formula bends in your favor. This is how professionals and high-net-worth borrowers unlock far more capital than the average homeowner ever realizes is available.

Practical Example: *How Optimization Increases a HELOC by Over $100,000*

Michael owns a home worth $650,000 and owes $380,000. At 80 percent CLTV, the maximum total debt is $520,000. Subtracting his mortgage leaves $140,000 as a HELOC. At 90 percent CLTV, the limit becomes $585,000. Subtracting $380,000 leaves $205,000. His credit score of 690 only qualifies him for 80 percent.

Michael improves his credit to 760 by paying down balances and correcting errors. Now he qualifies for 90 percent CLTV. His HELOC jumps from $140,000 to $205,000, a $65,000 increase.

He then switches to a lender that orders a full appraisal. His home appraises at $700,000. Ninety percent of $700,000 is $630,000. Subtracting his $380,000 mortgage leaves $250,000. He now has $110,000 more than when he started. This shows how optimization multiplies borrowing power.

Chapter 9

Risk, Reserves, and Bank Psychology: Why Some Borrowers Are Trusted With More

Once income, credit, debt, and home value are calculated, lenders apply a final layer of analysis that most borrowers never see. This layer is risk assessment. Risk is not just the chance that you will miss a payment; it is the chance that the lender will not be able to recover their money if something goes wrong. This is where reserves, savings, assets, and overall financial profile come into play. Two borrowers with identical income, credit, and homes can receive very different HELOC offers based on how much cash and liquidity they have available.

Reserves are the amount of money you have left over after closing, usually measured in months of mortgage payments. If your total housing payment is $3,000 per month and you have $18,000 in savings, you have six months of reserves. Many HELOC lenders require at least two to six months of reserves. Some allow more leverage for borrowers with higher reserves. The logic is simple: a borrower with cash in the bank is less likely to default during a temporary hardship. Banks also evaluate the stability of your assets. Money in a checking account, savings account, brokerage account, or retirement fund all count as assets. Even if those funds are not used for the loan, they serve as a cushion. A borrower with $200,000 in liquid assets is seen as far safer than one with $5,000, even if their income and credit are the same.

This is where wealthier borrowers often gain access to larger HELOCs and better rates. They are not just borrowing against a house; they are borrowing against their entire financial profile. Lenders want borrowers who can weather storms. That is why asset-based borrowers, retirees with large portfolios, and business owners with strong cash positions often qualify more easily than their income alone would suggest.

Another part of risk is employment and income stability. A ten-year employee at a stable company is seen as less risky than someone who started a new job last month. A business that has been profitable for five years is safer than one that launched last year. Time reduces perceived risk. This is why borrowers who wait a few months or years before applying often get much better terms.

Finally, lenders look at how leveraged you already are. Someone with multiple mortgages and HELOCs may still qualify, but only if their income, assets, and cash flow justify it. This is why professional borrowers keep careful balance sheets. They want to look strong not just on one loan, but across all of them.

Practical Example: *How Reserves and Assets Change HELOC Approval*

Thomas owns a home worth $600,000 and owes $350,000. At 85 percent CLTV, the maximum total debt is $510,000. Subtracting his mortgage leaves $160,000 as a possible HELOC. His income is $90,000 per year, or $7,500 per month. His mortgage is $2,400, his car is $500, and his credit cards are $300, totaling $3,200. A $160,000 HELOC at 8 percent creates a $1,067 payment. His total debt is $4,267. Dividing by $7,500 gives 57 percent DTI, which is too high.

However, Thomas has $200,000 in savings and investments. The lender allows asset depletion income. They divide his $200,000 by 60 months, adding $3,333 per month to his income. His new qualifying income becomes $10,833. Dividing $4,267 by $10,833 gives 39 percent. He now qualifies. His assets turned a denial into a six-figure HELOC approval.

Chapter 10

From Application to Approval: The Exact Path Your HELOC Takes Through the Bank

Many borrowers believe that once they submit a HELOC application, the rest is out of their hands. In reality, the underwriting process is where approvals are won or lost. Understanding what happens behind the scenes allows you to control delays, prevent mistakes, and avoid unnecessary denials. A HELOC file passes through several distinct stages: intake, verification, valuation, underwriting, conditions, and final approval. Each stage is governed by rules that determine whether the bank will trust you with access to your home equity.

The intake stage is where your information is first entered into the lender's system. This includes your income, debts, assets, credit profile, and property details. Errors at this stage are one of the most common reasons for denial. A misreported income, missing asset, or incorrect mortgage balance can make an otherwise approvable borrower appear unqualified. Professional borrowers review everything carefully before submission to ensure the numbers match their documents. The verification stage is where the bank proves that everything you stated is real. They verify income through pay stubs, tax returns, bank statements, or third-party services. They verify employment. They verify your mortgage balance. They verify your assets. Any discrepancy between what you claimed and what is verified triggers risk flags. Clean documentation leads to faster approvals and higher limits.

The valuation stage determines how much equity exists. This may involve an automated valuation, a drive-by appraisal, or a full interior appraisal. If the value comes in low, your HELOC limit drops automatically. Strategic borrowers prepare their homes, choose the right lenders, and challenge low valuations when needed.

Underwriting is where the full financial picture is analyzed. The underwriter calculates income, debts, DTI, CLTV, credit risk, and reserves. If anything is marginal, they may issue conditions, which are requests for more documents or explanations. This is not a denial; it is an opportunity to strengthen the file. How these conditions are answered often determines whether the HELOC is approved and for how much.

Once all conditions are cleared, the file moves to final approval and closing. Funds become available only after documents are signed and recorded. Borrowers who understand this process avoid surprises and get better results.

Practical Example: *How the Underwriting Process Produces a Final HELOC Approval*

Karen owns a home valued at $620,000 and owes $340,000. The bank allows 85 percent CLTV. $620,000 multiplied by 0.85 equals $527,000. Subtracting her mortgage leaves $187,000 as the maximum possible HELOC.

Karen earns $100,000 per year, or $8,333 per month. Her debts are $2,400 mortgage, $600 car, and $300 credit cards, totaling $3,300. The HELOC payment on $187,000 at 8 percent is $1,247. Her total debt becomes $4,547. Dividing $4,547 by $8,333 gives 54 percent DTI, which is too high.

Karen submits $50,000 in savings. The bank allows asset income by dividing this by 60 months, adding $833 per month. Her income becomes $9,166. Now $4,547 divided by $9,166 equals 49.6 percent. She qualifies. After underwriting, Karen receives a $187,000 HELOC.

Chapter 11

Denials, Appeals, and Second Chances: How to Turn a "No" Into a "Yes"

A HELOC denial is not the end of the road; it is simply a data point. Most borrowers treat a denial as final, but professional borrowers treat it as feedback. Every denial comes with a reason, even if it is not clearly explained. Those reasons always fall into one of four categories: equity, income, debt, or credit. Once you identify which number caused the denial, you can change it. This is why understanding the qualification formula gives you power even after you are told no.

Lenders are required to provide adverse action notices explaining why a loan was denied. These notices may list reasons such as "excessive obligations," "insufficient income," "limited equity," or "credit risk." Each of these corresponds to a specific mathematical limit inside the underwriting model. "Excessive obligations" means your DTI was too high. "Insufficient income" means your documented income was too low. "Limited equity" means CLTV exceeded the lender's maximum. "Credit risk" means your score, utilization, or recent history triggered a cap. These are not vague judgments; they are numbers that missed a threshold. Appeals are one of the most underused tools in lending. Many HELOC lenders allow borrowers to submit additional documentation or explanations to overcome a denial. For example, if income was too low, updated pay stubs, bank statements, or asset statements may change the calculation. If value was too low, new comparable sales or a reconsideration of value may increase the appraisal. If credit was the issue, paying down balances and re-pulling credit can change the result within weeks.

Some denials are lender-specific. One bank's rules are not another's. A borrower denied at a conservative credit union may be approved at a portfolio lender that allows higher DTIs or different income documentation. This is why working with multiple lenders or a broker gives you far more leverage than applying blindly to one bank.

Denials also create strategy. If you know you were denied because your DTI was 48 percent and the lender's cap was 45 percent, you know exactly how much debt must be eliminated or income added to qualify. You are no longer guessing. You are solving an equation. This allows you to take precise actions that produce approval instead of random financial moves.

The most powerful borrowers are not those who never get denied. They are the ones who know how to convert a denial into a roadmap. That is how you turn frustration into control.

Practical Example: *Turning a HELOC Denial Into a Six-Figure Approval*

Jason owns a home worth $580,000. He owes $330,000. At 85 percent CLTV, the maximum total debt allowed is $580,000 multiplied by 0.85, which equals $493,000. Subtracting his $330,000 mortgage leaves $163,000 as a possible HELOC. Jason earns $95,000 per year, or $7,917 per month. His debts are $2,400 mortgage, $600 car, and $400 credit cards, totaling $3,400.

The HELOC payment on $163,000 at 8 percent is $1,087. Total monthly debt becomes $4,487. Dividing $4,487 by $7,917 gives 56.6 percent DTI. The lender's maximum is 45 percent, so Jason is denied for "excessive obligations."

Jason now knows exactly what to fix. To reach 45 percent DTI, his total debt must be no more than $7,917 multiplied by 0.45, which equals $3,562. His current debt is $4,487, so he must reduce it by $925. Jason pays off his $600 car loan and $400 of his credit cards, reducing his debt by $1,000. His new monthly debt is $3,487.

Now $3,487 divided by $7,917 equals 44 percent. Jason reapplies and is approved for the full $163,000 HELOC. This shows how denial is simply math waiting to be corrected.

Chapter 12

Your HELOC Readiness Blueprint: How to Know When You Are Guaranteed to Qualify

Most homeowners apply for a HELOC hoping they qualify. Professional borrowers apply when they already know they qualify. The difference is preparation. This chapter ties together every variable in the HELOC formula and shows you how to build a personal readiness blueprint that removes uncertainty from the process. When your blueprint is complete, approval is no longer a guess; it is the predictable result of numbers that already fit inside the lender's rules.

A HELOC readiness blueprint starts with equity. You must know what your home is worth, how your lender will value it, and what CLTV they allow. This gives you a hard ceiling on how much you can borrow. Without this number, you cannot plan income, debt, or credit strategy. When you know your maximum allowable loan, you can reverse-engineer everything else.

The second piece is income. You must know exactly how much qualifying income your lender will count. This may be your salary, your business net income, your bank statement deposits, your rental cash flow, or your assets. Once you know that number, you can calculate the maximum monthly payment you can support.

The third piece is debt. You list every monthly obligation that appears on your credit report and housing statement. You then subtract this from your allowable DTI threshold. This tells you how much room is left for a HELOC payment. If the HELOC payment for your target loan fits inside that number, you qualify. If it does not, you know exactly how much debt must be reduced or income increased.

The fourth piece is credit. Your score and profile determine whether you get the highest CLTV, the best rates, and the easiest approval. A readiness blueprint includes a plan to optimize utilization, eliminate late payments, and avoid new inquiries before applying.

When all four pieces are aligned, HELOC approval becomes automatic. You are no longer at the mercy of the bank. You are walking into the system already compliant with its rules. This is how professional borrowers consistently unlock large amounts of home equity while others are left confused and frustrated.

Practical Example: *Building a HELOC Readiness Blueprint*

Natalie owns a home worth $650,000 and owes $370,000. Her lender allows 85 percent CLTV. The maximum total debt allowed is $650,000 multiplied by 0.85, which equals $552,500. Subtracting her mortgage leaves $182,500 as the maximum HELOC.

Natalie earns $110,000 per year, or $9,167 per month. Her lender allows a maximum DTI of 45 percent. Forty-five percent of $9,167 equals $4,125. This means all her debts, including the HELOC, must be below $4,125 per month.

Natalie's current debts are a $2,500 mortgage, a $600 car payment, and $300 in credit cards, totaling $3,400. Subtracting $3,400 from her $4,125 limit leaves $725 available for a HELOC payment.

At 8 percent interest, a $182,500 HELOC has a payment of $1,217 per month, which is too high. Natalie reduces her debt by paying off her car loan, lowering her debt by $600. Now her debt is $2,800, leaving $1,325 for a HELOC payment. This supports the full $182,500 line. Natalie applies and is approved. This is what readiness looks like.

Chapter 13

From Borrower to Power User: How to Use Your First HELOC to Qualify for Bigger Ones

Most homeowners see HELOC approval as the finish line. In reality, it is the starting line. Once you have one HELOC, you enter a different financial category in the eyes of lenders. You now have a revolving credit facility secured by real estate, and how you use it will determine whether banks see you as disciplined and scalable or risky and maxed out. This chapter explains how to use your first HELOC strategically so it becomes a stepping stone to larger lines, better terms, and more borrowing power across your financial life.

When a lender issues a HELOC, they are not just lending money; they are evaluating how you manage access to capital. Revolving credit lines are powerful indicators of borrower behavior. If you draw small amounts, pay them back, keep balances low, and never miss payments, your profile strengthens. If you max out the line, carry high balances, and show erratic usage, your risk profile rises. Lenders who review your credit later will see not just that you have a HELOC, but how you used it. One of the most important metrics is utilization. HELOCs report to credit bureaus like other revolving lines. If you have a $150,000 HELOC and you are using $10,000, your utilization is under 7 percent, which looks excellent. If you are using $120,000, your utilization is 80 percent, which looks risky even if you make payments. Low utilization signals control. High utilization signals dependency. This directly affects your credit score and your ability to qualify for additional HELOCs or higher limits.

Payment history on a HELOC also carries significant weight. Because HELOCs are secured by real estate, late payments are taken very seriously by lenders. Even one late HELOC payment can eliminate access to future home equity products for years. On-time payments, on the other hand, build a powerful record of trust. After twelve months of perfect HELOC history, many borrowers find it much easier to qualify for increases or new lines.

How you deploy HELOC funds also matters. Using a HELOC to eliminate high-interest debt, invest in cash-flowing assets, or improve your property strengthens your financial profile. Using it for consumption, vacations, or depreciating purchases does not. Lenders are not tracking what you spend on directly, but they see the results in your balance sheet and cash flow. Borrowers who use HELOCs to improve their net worth and income look safer over time. Once a HELOC is established and managed properly, it can be used to create new equity. For example, using HELOC funds to renovate a property can increase its value, creating more borrowing capacity. Using it as a down payment for another property creates another asset that can later support its own HELOC. This is how professional real estate investors build large portfolios without constantly injecting new cash.

The key to becoming a power user is discipline. The HELOC is not free money; it is a leverage tool. When used correctly, it increases wealth and borrowing power. When used poorly, it reduces both. This chapter teaches you how to stay on the right side of that line so your first HELOC becomes the foundation for a much larger financial future.

Practical Example: *How One HELOC Becomes Three*

Daniel owns a home worth $600,000 and owes $320,000. At 85 percent CLTV, his maximum total debt is $510,000. Subtracting his mortgage leaves $190,000. He is approved for a $190,000 HELOC. Daniel uses only $40,000 of it to pay off credit cards and make a $40,000 down payment on a rental property. His HELOC balance is now $80,000. His utilization is $80,000 divided by $190,000, which equals 42 percent. Over the next year, he pays it down to $30,000. His utilization drops to 16 percent. Because Daniel's HELOC payments are on time and his balances are low, his credit score increases. His rental property appreciates to $300,000 with a $200,000 mortgage. At 80 percent CLTV, that property supports $240,000 in total debt. Subtracting $200,000 leaves $40,000. Daniel now qualifies for a second HELOC.

Meanwhile, Daniel's original home appreciates to $650,000. At 85 percent CLTV, that allows $552,500 in total debt. Subtracting his $320,000 mortgage and $30,000 HELOC balance leaves $202,500. He increases his HELOC from $190,000 to $202,500. Daniel now has three equity lines across two properties, all because he managed the first one correctly.

Chapter 14

The Long-Term Qualification Strategy: How to Keep Qualifying for Bigger HELOCs for Life

Most people think qualifying for a HELOC is a one-time event. In reality, it is a lifelong financial skill. Every HELOC you get, every refinance you complete, every mortgage you pay down, and every asset you acquire changes how lenders see you. Borrowers who understand this treat their balance sheet like a living system that is always being prepared for the next round of capital. This chapter explains how to structure your finances so you never lose access to home equity and continuously qualify for larger and better HELOCs over time.

The foundation of long-term HELOC eligibility is equity growth. Equity grows in two ways: through market appreciation and through principal paydown. When your home increases in value or your mortgage balance decreases, your available borrowing power rises. Strategic borrowers accelerate both. They choose properties in appreciating areas, they make smart upgrades that increase value, and they make extra principal payments when it makes sense. Even small increases in equity compound over time. On a $600,000 home, a 5 percent appreciation adds $30,000 in value. At 85 percent CLTV, that creates more than $25,000 in new HELOC capacity.

The second pillar is income stability and growth. Lenders do not want borrowers who peak and then decline. They want borrowers who show upward or at least steady financial trajectories. This means maintaining stable employment, growing a business in a documented way, increasing rents on rental properties, or building investment income. When your income grows, your DTI capacity grows, allowing you to qualify for larger HELOCs even if your balances also grow.

The third pillar is debt control. Long-term HELOC power requires that you avoid becoming over-leveraged. Every loan you take reduces future borrowing capacity unless it also creates income or value. Strategic borrowers use HELOCs to replace bad debt with good debt. They eliminate high-interest consumer debt, then use leverage to acquire or improve assets that increase income or equity. This keeps their DTI and CLTV in balance as their portfolio grows.

The fourth pillar is credit discipline. Your credit profile is your financial reputation. Late payments, high utilization, and reckless borrowing can destroy HELOC access for years. On the other hand, disciplined use of revolving credit, including HELOCs, builds a powerful record of trust. Long-term borrowers keep utilization low, pay on time, and avoid unnecessary inquiries. Over time, this unlocks higher CLTVs, better rates, and easier approvals.

When these four pillars are managed together, HELOC qualification becomes self-reinforcing. Equity creates borrowing power. Borrowing power creates opportunities. Opportunities create income and value. Income and value create more equity. This is the wealth cycle that banks are built around. Most people never learn it. Those who do can access millions of dollars in capital over their lifetime without ever needing investors or partners.

Practical Example: *How One Home Becomes a Lifetime Capital Machine*

Rachel buys a home for $500,000 with a $400,000 mortgage. Five years later, the home is worth $650,000 and she owes $360,000. At 85 percent CLTV, her maximum total debt is $552,500. Subtracting $360,000 leaves $192,500. She qualifies for her first HELOC.

Rachel uses $50,000 from the HELOC to renovate the home. The renovation increases the home's value to $720,000. At 85 percent CLTV, the maximum total debt is now $612,000. Subtracting her $360,000 mortgage and her $50,000 HELOC balance leaves $202,000 in remaining equity. Her borrowing capacity has grown instead of shrinking.

Over the next five years, Rachel pays her mortgage down to $300,000 and her home appreciates to $800,000. Eighty-five percent of $800,000 is $680,000. Subtracting $300,000 and her $50,000 HELOC balance leaves $330,000. Rachel now has over $330,000 in available HELOC capacity on the same house. By managing equity, debt, income, and credit properly, she turned one home into a lifelong financial engine.

Chapter 15

The Ultimate HELOC Qualification System: How to Engineer Your Financial Life for Unlimited Access to Capital

Most homeowners approach HELOCs as isolated financial products. Professional borrowers approach them as part of a lifelong capital system. The difference between these two mindsets determines whether home equity becomes a short-term cash source or a permanent wealth-building engine. This chapter brings together every lesson from this book into a single operating system you can use to continually qualify for larger, better, and more flexible HELOCs throughout your life.

At the core of the HELOC qualification system is understanding that banks lend against balance sheets, not people. They evaluate four categories every time: equity, income, debt, and credit. Your job as a professional borrower is to manage all four categories in a way that always keeps you inside lender thresholds. When these variables are in balance, you qualify easily. When one drifts out of alignment, approvals stop. Treating these numbers as living variables instead of fixed facts gives you control. Equity is the foundation of the system. Every mortgage payment you make and every increase in home value adds to your borrowing power. But equity only becomes useful when it is recognized by a lender through valuation. This means choosing properties in strong markets, making improvements that raise appraised value, and periodically re-appraising or refinancing to reset your CLTV. You are not just building a home; you are building a financial asset designed to support capital access.

Income is the fuel of the system. Lenders must see that you can service the debt. Professional borrowers structure their income in ways that maximize what can be documented. They understand how W-2 income, self-employment income, rental income, and asset-based income are calculated. They time applications after strong financial periods and avoid applying when income is temporarily low. Over time, they build multiple income streams that create more and more borrowing capacity.

Debt is the control lever. Every monthly payment reduces your available DTI. Professional borrowers are not anti-debt; they are anti-bad-debt. They eliminate high-interest consumer obligations and replace them with low-interest, asset-backed leverage. This keeps their total payments manageable while their assets and income grow. When debt creates income or appreciation, it strengthens rather than weakens future

HELOC eligibility. Credit is the reputation layer. Your credit profile tells lenders how you handle leverage. Low utilization, long account history, and perfect payment records lead to higher CLTVs and lower rates. Reckless borrowing does the opposite. HELOC power users treat their credit like a financial résumé that must always look professional.

When these four components are managed together, something powerful happens. Every improvement in one area strengthens the others. More income supports more debt. More debt used wisely creates more assets. More assets create more equity. More equity allows larger HELOCs. Larger HELOCs allow more investment. This compounding cycle is how wealthy borrowers use home equity to create long-term financial dominance.

Practical Example: *Engineering a Lifetime of HELOC Power*

Anthony buys a home for $450,000 with a $360,000 mortgage. Five years later, the home is worth $600,000 and he owes $330,000. At 85 percent CLTV, the maximum total debt allowed is $600,000 multiplied by 0.85, which equals $510,000. Subtracting $330,000 leaves $180,000. He is approved for a $180,000 HELOC.

Anthony uses $60,000 of the HELOC to renovate the home and $40,000 as a down payment on a rental property. His HELOC balance becomes $100,000. The renovation increases the home's value to $700,000. Eighty-five percent of $700,000 is $595,000. Subtracting his $330,000 mortgage and $100,000 HELOC balance leaves $165,000 in remaining equity. Even after borrowing, his capacity is higher than when he started.

The rental property is worth $250,000 with a $200,000 mortgage. At 80 percent CLTV, it supports $200,000. Anthony later refinances and qualifies for a $40,000 HELOC on the rental. He now has $205,000 in total HELOC access across two properties. His income increases from rental cash flow, improving his DTI and allowing even more borrowing. This is how one HELOC becomes a permanent capital system.

Final Thoughts

Qualifying for a HELOC is not about luck, timing, or who you happen to talk to at a bank. It is about understanding how a financial system works and positioning yourself inside that system. Throughout this book, you have seen that every approval, every limit, and every rate comes from the same underlying formula: equity, income, debt, credit, and risk. Once you understand how those pieces fit together, you stop being a passive borrower and become a strategic one. That shift is the most important outcome of this book.

Most homeowners never learn these rules. They assume that lenders make subjective decisions or that approvals are mysterious. In reality, banks are running numbers. They are measuring how much risk you represent, how much equity protects them, and how stable your financial life appears. When you know that, every financial decision you make becomes more intentional. You begin to see how paying down one loan, improving one credit account, or waiting one extra month before applying can change the outcome by tens or even hundreds of thousands of dollars.

This book was written to give you control over that outcome. You now know how your home is valued, how your income is counted, how your debts affect your borrowing power, and how your credit profile influences not only whether you are approved but how much access you receive. You have also seen how lenders use reserves, assets, and overall financial stability to decide how much they trust you. These are not abstract ideas. They are the real rules that govern how much capital you can unlock from your home.

What makes a HELOC so powerful is not just that it gives you access to cash. It gives you access to flexibility. A HELOC can be used to eliminate high-interest debt, smooth cash flow, invest in opportunities, improve properties, or simply provide financial security. But that power only exists if you can qualify for the right amount at the right terms. That is why this book matters. It is not about borrowing; it is about positioning.

One of the most important lessons in this book is that qualification is something you can prepare for. You do not have to apply and hope. You can measure your own numbers, calculate your own DTI, estimate your own equity, and understand your own credit profile before you ever submit an application. When you do that, the process becomes predictable. You know when you are ready. You know what needs to change if you are not. That puts you in a position of strength instead of uncertainty. You have also seen how HELOCs fit into a larger financial strategy. The goal is not just to get one line of credit. The goal is to build a financial profile that allows you to access capital whenever you need it. That means growing equity, stabilizing income, controlling debt, and protecting your credit over time. When you manage those four elements together, your home becomes more than a place to live. It becomes a financial engine that supports your goals for decades.

This book is only the beginning of that journey. In the rest of the Home Equity Wealth Series, you will see how to use HELOCs to eliminate debt, fund investments, build businesses, manage risk, and create long-term financial stability. But none of that is possible without the foundation you have built here. Qualification is the gateway to everything that comes next.

As a licensed mortgage broker, I can tell you that the borrowers who succeed with home equity are not the ones who take the most risk. They are the ones who understand the system and use it deliberately. They know their numbers. They know their limits. They know when to act and when to wait. That is what you now have as well.

Your home already contains tremendous financial potential. The only question is whether you know how to unlock it. After reading this book, you do.

How to Get a Personalized HELOC Review

If you found *HELOC Fundamentals: How Home Equity Lines of Credit Really Work — and How to Use Them Safely* helpful, you may want to see how these concepts apply to your own home, credit profile, and financial goals.

Every homeowner's situation is unique. Home value, mortgage balance, credit history, income type, and state-specific lending rules all affect how much equity you can access, what type of HELOC you may qualify for, and what terms may be available. The examples in this book are designed to teach how HELOCs work — but your real options can only be determined by reviewing your actual numbers.

If you would like a **no-obligation Home Equity Line of Credit review**, you can request one here:

Website:https://www.nodocsheloc.com

Email:info@FinibiMortgage.com

A licensed mortgage broker will review your information and explain what HELOC and home equity options may be available to you based on your specific situation.

No cost. No pressure. No obligation.

Joseph G. Correa

About the Author

Joseph G. Correa is a licensed mortgage broker and the founder of Finibi Mortgage, a Florida-based brokerage specializing in home equity, real estate investment financing, and alternative lending strategies for homeowners, business owners, and investors. With more than two decades of experience in mortgage lending, underwriting, and financial structuring, Joseph has helped thousands of borrowers access capital using intelligent, low-risk leverage rather than high-interest consumer debt.

Unlike traditional loan officers who focus only on closing transactions, Joseph's approach is rooted in long-term financial strategy. He believes that mortgages, HELOCs, and credit lines should be used as tools for building wealth, protecting cash flow, and creating financial resilience — not as traps that keep families locked into decades of unnecessary interest payments. This philosophy has made him a trusted advisor for entrepreneurs, real estate investors, and self-employed borrowers who need flexible, modern financing solutions that banks often fail to provide.

Joseph is widely known for his expertise in home equity lines of credit, no-documentation and bank-statement loan programs, investor financing, and creative equity-based strategies such as debt-elimination systems and capital recycling. His ability to translate complex lending rules into simple, actionable guidance has helped homeowners turn idle equity into productive capital for investments, businesses, and passive income.

Through his education platform, Finibi Academy, Joseph has trained tens of thousands of students worldwide in credit, mortgage strategy, real estate financing, and financial independence. His courses and books are used by first-time homeowners, seasoned investors, and financial professionals seeking a clearer, more honest understanding of how modern lending really works.

Joseph created *The Home Equity Wealth Series* to give everyday homeowners the same financial knowledge that banks, hedge funds, and institutional investors use to control capital and minimize risk. His mission is simple: to help people stop guessing, stop fearing debt, and start using smart leverage to build real financial freedom.

When he is not structuring loans or writing, Joseph works with families and investors across the United States to design personalized equity strategies that align with their goals, cash flow, and long-term wealth plans.

The Home Equity Wealth Series Roadmap

The Professional Guide to Using Your Home to Build Financial Freedom

The purpose of *The Home Equity Wealth Series* is to give homeowners the same financial tools and strategies used by banks, investors, and institutions—translated into clear, practical guidance for everyday people. Each book builds on the last, taking you from basic understanding to advanced mastery of how to use home equity safely, intelligently, and profitably across every stage of life.

Book 1 — *HELOC Fundamentals*This book gives you the foundation. You will understand how Home Equity Lines of Credit work, how they are structured, how risk is controlled, and how equity becomes usable capital. The books that follow are designed to help you apply that knowledge to your own situation, your income type, your credit profile, and your long-term financial goals.

Book 2 — *How to Qualify for a HELOC* This book shows you how lenders actually evaluate borrowers. You will learn how credit scores, income, property type, and debt ratios affect approval, limits, and interest rates. You will also learn how to position yourself to qualify for the largest possible credit line at the best possible terms.

Book 3 – *HELOCs for Real Estate Investors* This book focuses on using home equity to buy, rehab, refinance, and scale rental properties. It explains how investors use HELOCs for down payments, renovations, and portfolio growth while keeping cash flow positive and risk controlled.

Book 4 – *Self-Employed HELOC Strategies* Designed for business owners, freelancers, 1099 borrowers, and LLCs, this book explains how bank-statement income, business income, and alternative documentation can be used to qualify for home equity even when traditional tax returns do not reflect true cash flow.

Book 5 – *Credit Mastery for HELOC Approval* This book dives deep into credit strategy. You will learn how utilization, credit mix, and reporting behavior affect HELOC limits and pricing—and how to optimize your credit profile specifically for home equity approval.

Book 6 – *No-Doc & Alternative HELOC Programs* This book covers asset-based HELOCs, no-income-verification options, and non-traditional lending programs for high-net-worth, self-employed, or cash-heavy borrowers who do not fit inside standard underwriting models.

Book 7 – *Using a HELOC to Eliminate Debt* This book teaches how to use home equity to replace high-interest credit cards, personal loans, and auto loans with low-interest revolving credit, allowing borrowers to eliminate debt years faster and save tens of thousands of dollars in interest.

Book 8 — *Using a HELOC to Build Wealth* This book shows how homeowners fund investments, businesses, and passive income streams using HELOCs while maintaining liquidity and controlling risk.

Book 9 — *HELOC Risk Management* This book focuses entirely on safety. You will learn how to structure buffers, cash-flow coverage, rate protection, and leverage limits so your home becomes safer over time—not more vulnerable.

Book 10 — *The Smart Borrower's Home Equity Blueprint* The final book ties everything together into a complete lifetime strategy for using home equity as a personal banking system, investment engine, and financial safety net.

Book 11 — *The Cashflow Accelerator Method*

The Cashflow Accelerator Method is the final transformation stage of *The Home Equity Wealth Series.* While the earlier books teach how to access, qualify for, and safely use home equity, this book teaches how to **weaponize cash flow itself** to permanently eliminate debt and create lasting wealth. Together, these books are designed to turn a single asset—your home—into a lifelong financial advantage. Each volume adds another layer of understanding, allowing you to move from homeowner to capital manager, from borrower to strategist, and from financial stress to long-term stability.

This is not about taking more risk.It is about learning how money really works—and using that knowledge to build financial freedom that lasts.

Educational & Financial Disclaimer

This book is provided for **educational and informational purposes only**. The author and publisher are not engaged in rendering legal, tax, accounting, investment, or financial advice. Although the author is a licensed mortgage broker, the information in this book is intended to provide general education about Home Equity Lines of Credit (HELOCs) and home equity strategy, not personalized financial, legal, or lending advice.

Mortgage programs, underwriting guidelines, interest rates, credit requirements, and home equity products vary by lender, investor, state, and economic conditions, and may change at any time without notice. The examples, calculations, and scenarios presented in this book are hypothetical and are for illustration only. They do not represent guaranteed outcomes or actual loan approvals.

Before making any financial decisions, including applying for a HELOC, refinancing, borrowing against home equity, or using credit for investment or debt repayment, readers should consult with a qualified mortgage professional, financial advisor, tax advisor, or attorney who can evaluate their specific situation.

Risk Disclosure

Borrowing against home equity involves risk. A HELOC is secured by your home, which means failure to make required payments could result in foreclosure or loss of property. This book teaches responsible, conservative, and structured use of home equity, but no financial strategy is risk-free.

Readers are solely responsible for their financial decisions. Neither the author nor the publisher makes any warranties, express or implied, about the accuracy, completeness, or applicability of the information in this book to any individual or situation.

www.ingramcontent.com/pod-product-compliance
Lightning Source LLC
LaVergne TN
LVHW022023200926
848481LV00007B/2511
* 9 7 9 8 2 9 5 5 7 3 9 0 3 *